CHRISTMAS CAROLS

ILLUSTRATED BY
NOEL TENNYSON

RANDOM HOUSE 🏠 NEW YORK

Copyright © 1981 by Random House, Inc.
All rights reserved under International and Pan-American Copyright Conventions.
Published in the United States by Random House, Inc., New York,
and simultaneously in Canada by Random House of Canada Limited, Toronto.
Library of Congress Catalog Card Number: 83-60412   ISBN: 0-394-86125-6
Manufactured in the United States of America
8 9 0

DECK THE HALLS

Deck the halls with boughs of holly,
Fa la la la la, la la la la.
'Tis the season to be jolly,
Fa la la la la, la la la la.
Don we now our gay apparel,
Fa la la, la la la, la la la.
Toll the ancient yuletide carol,
Fa la la la la, la la la la.

Fast away the old year passes,
Fa la la . . .
Hail the new, ye lads and lasses,
Fa la la . . .
Sing we joyous all together,
Fa la la . . .
Heedless of the wind and weather,
Fa la la . . .

WE THREE KINGS OF ORIENT ARE

We three kings of Orient are;
Bearing gifts, we traverse afar,
Field and fountain, moor and mountain,
Following yonder star.

O star of wonder, star of night,
Star with royal beauty bright,
Westward leading still proceeding,
Guide us to Thy perfect light.

Born a King on Bethlehem's plain,
Gold we bring, to crown Him again,
King forever, ceasing never
Over us all to reign.

O Come, All Ye Faithful

O come, all ye faithful,
Joyful and triumphant,
O come ye, O come ye to Bethlehem;
Come and behold Him,
Born the King of angels;
O come, let us adore Him,
O come, let us adore Him,
O come, let us adore Him,
Christ the Lord.

Sing, choirs of angels,
Sing in exultation,
Sing, all ye citizens of heav'n above!
"Glory to God.
All glory in the highest!"
O come, let us adore Him,
O come, let us adore Him,
O come, let us adore Him,
Christ the Lord.

WE WISH YOU A MERRY CHRISTMAS

We wish you a merry Christmas,
We wish you a merry Christmas,
We wish you a merry Christmas,
And a happy New Year!

Good tidings to you, wherever you are,
Good tidings for Christmas and a happy New Year!

We'd all like some cake and candy,
We'd all like some cake and candy,
We'd all like some cake and candy,
So bring it right here.

We won't go until we get some,
We won't go until we get some,
We won't go until we get some,
With a smile of good cheer.

O LITTLE TOWN OF BETHLEHEM

O little town of Bethlehem,
How still we see thee lie.
Above thy deep and dreamless sleep
The silent stars go by;
Yet in thy dark streets shineth
The everlasting Light;
The hopes and fears of all the years
Are met in thee tonight.

For Christ is born of Mary;
And gathered all above,
While mortals sleep, the angels keep
Their watch of wond'ring love.
O morning stars together
Proclaim the holy birth,
And praises sing to God the King,
And peace to men on earth!

AWAY IN A MANGER

Away in a manger, no crib for a bed,
The little Lord Jesus laid down His sweet head.
The stars in the sky looked down where He lay,
The little Lord Jesus, asleep on the hay.

The cattle are lowing, the Baby awakes,
But little Lord Jesus, no crying He makes.
I love Thee, Lord Jesus, look down from the sky,
And stay by my cradle till morning is nigh.

HARK! THE HERALD ANGELS SING

Hark! The herald angels sing,
"Glory to the newborn King;
Peace on earth, and mercy mild,
God and sinners reconciled!"
Joyful all ye nations rise,
Join the triumph of the skies;
With th'angelic host proclaim,
"Christ is born in Bethlehem!"
Hark! The herald angels sing,
"Glory to the newborn King."

JOY TO THE WORLD

Joy to the world! The Lord is come;
Let earth receive her King;
Let every heart, prepare Him room,
And heaven and nature sing,
And heaven and nature sing,
And heaven, and heaven and nature sing.

Joy to the earth! The Savior reigns;
Let men their songs employ;
While fields and floods, rocks, hills, and plains,
Repeat the sounding joy,
Repeat the sounding joy,
Repeat, repeat the sounding joy.

He rules the world with truth and grace,
And makes the nations prove
The glories of His righteousness,
And wonders of His love,
And wonders of His love,
And wonders, wonders of His love.

O CHRISTMAS TREE

O Christmas tree, O Christmas tree,
With faithful leaves unchanging;
O Christmas tree, O Christmas tree,
With faithful leaves unchanging;
Not only green in summer's heat,
But also winter's snow and sleet,
O Christmas tree, O Christmas tree,
With faithful leaves unchanging.

O Christmas tree, O Christmas tree,
Of all the trees most lovely . . .
Each year you bring me to delight
Gleaming in the Christmas light.
O Christmas tree, O Christmas tree.
Of all the trees most lovely.

SILENT NIGHT

Silent night! Holy night!
All is calm, all is bright,
'Round yon virgin Mother and Child.
Holy infant so tender and mild,
Sleep in heavenly peace,
Sleep in heavenly peace!

Silent night! Holy night!
Shepherds quake at the sight,
Glories stream from heaven afar,
Heavenly hosts sing *alleluia*;
Christ, the Savior, is born,
Christ, the Savior, is born!